D0345571

GINGER BREAD

WONDERLAND

FOR TOM

When your tummy rumbles at teatime,
it's natures way of telling you to eat more cookies.

GINGER BREAD
WONDERLAND

30 MAGICAL COOKIES, CAKES & HOUSES

★ MIMA SINCLAIR ★

An Hachette UK Company
www.hachette.co.uk

First published in Great Britain in 2015 by
Kyle Books, an imprint of Kyle Cathie Ltd
Carmelite House
50 Victoria Embankment
London EC4Y 0DZ
www.kylebooks.co.uk

This edition published in 2019

ISBN: 978 0 85783 756 1

Text © 2015 Mima Sinclair
Design © 2015 Kyle Books
Photographs © 2015 Tara Fisher

Distributed in the US by Hachette Book Group, 1290 Avenue
of the Americas, 4th and 5th Floors, New York, NY 10104

Distributed in Canada by Canadian Manda Group, 664 Annette
St., Toronto, Ontario, Canada M6S 2C8

Mima Sinclair is hereby identified as the author of this work
in accordance with section 77 of the Copyright, Designs and
Patents Act 1988.

All rights reserved. No part of this work may be reproduced or
utilised in any form or by any means, electronic or mechanical,
including photocopying, recording or by any information storage
and retrieval system, without the prior written permission of
the publisher.

Designer: Anita Mangan
Photographer: Tara Fisher
Food Stylist: Mima Sinclair
Prop Stylist: Tabitha Hawkins
Project Editor: Sophie Allen
Editorial Assistant: Hannah Coughlin
Americanizer: Christy Lusiak
Production: Nic Jones, Gemma John, and Lisa Pinnell

Printed and bound in China

10 9 8 7 6 5 4 3 2 1

CONTENTS

INTRODUCTION

I love baking. My knees go weak at the sight of a chewy cookie or a light, airy cake. More frosting goes in my mouth than makes it onto its intended counterpart. I blame my mother—she spoiled us with homemade cookies and treats after school. Coming home to a house still full of the heady scent of baked goods is something that doesn't leave you. Friends at school would always want to come to our house on the weekend because the kitchen wasn't banned, it was our playground.

So my love affair with sweet treats has grown up with me, it's molded me, it's comforted me, and the comfort I have felt has happily spread to others. That's the joy of baking—people are thrilled by it. I like to feed those around me with all the sweet delights that I get so much excitement out of baking, and they eagerly receive them. I get just as much joy from sharing goodies as I do gobbling them all up myself!

This collection of recipes has something for everyone's tastes and suits a variety of baking abilities. Packed with a range of classic and contemporary recipes, you have all you need to turn your kitchen into a gingerbread wonderland. Bake perfect treats to slip into lunch boxes, serve up to friends in the afternoon, give as gifts, or have as a festive centerpiece. Show up at a party with a gingerbread house and you are sure to be at the top of everyone's invite lists next year!

I hate recipes that need lots of complicated equipment and hard-to-source ingredients. The ingredients used in these recipes are basic and inexpensive, as are the little bits of equipment you will need along the way. Most of these things you will probably already have in your pantry, but please heed my advice in the dough tips about old spices. New cutters don't have to be bought—use what you have or create your own from thick cardstock, using my templates (see pages 96 to 109).

Follow my tips on dough, baking, and piping to avoid mistakes and achieve your best-ever baked treats. A word of advice—don't sweat the small stuff. Who cares if your piping isn't straight, your gingerbread house is crooked, or something didn't turn out exactly the way you meant it—mine doesn't always and that's the magic of it being homemade. I guarantee your efforts will still be met with wide, greedy eyes and you will soon enjoy the beautiful silence that only comes from a room of contented people whose mouths are full. Now get in the kitchen and have some fun!

LIGHT GINGERBREAD DOUGH

MAKES 2¼ POUNDS · PREP: 10 MINUTES, PLUS 1 HOUR 15 MINUTES CHILLING · COOK: 5 MINUTES

This is a mild and sweet, light dough that is very versatile.

½ cup light molasses, golden syrup, or honey

1 cup light brown sugar

14 tablespoons (1 stick + 6 tablespoons) unsalted butter

zest of 1 lemon

4 teaspoons ground ginger

2 teaspoons ground cinnamon

½ teaspoon ground nutmeg

¼ teaspoon ground cloves

1 teaspoon baking soda

4 cups all-purpose flour

1 teaspoon salt

1 lightly beaten large free-range egg

1. Pour the light molasses into a large saucepan with the sugar, butter, zest, and spices and melt over low/medium heat, stirring frequently until the sugar has dissolved.

2. Increase the heat to bring the mixture to boiling point. Remove from the heat and beat in the baking soda. The mixture will froth up at this point as the baking soda reacts—mix briefly until combined, then let cool for 15 minutes.

3. Sift the flour and salt, then fold into the mixture in batches, using a wooden spoon or a stand mixer. Beat in the egg using a wooden spoon or a stand mixer, until just combined. Do not overwork the mixture, or the cookies will spread during baking.

4. The dough will be very sticky to begin with, but do not add any flour. Scrape out of the bowl onto a clean surface and knead together until just smooth. Wrap in plastic wrap and chill in the fridge for 1 hour.

DARK
GINGERBREAD DOUGH

MAKES 2¼ POUNDS · PREP: 10 MINUTES, PLUS 1 HOUR 15 MINUTES CHILLING · COOK: 5 MINUTES

A stronger, spicier dough and visually darker because of the use of dark molasses.

¼ cup dark molasses/
black treacle

3 tablespoons light
molasses, golden
syrup, or honey

1 cup dark brown sugar

14 tablespoons (1 stick +
6 tablespoons) unsalted
butter

zest of ½ orange

4 teaspoons ground
ginger

2 teaspoons
ground cinnamon

½ teaspoon
ground nutmeg

¼ teaspoon
ground cloves

1 teaspoon baking soda

4 cups all-purpose flour

1 teaspoon salt

1 lightly beaten large
free-range egg

1. Pour the dark and light molasses into a large saucepan with the sugar, butter, zest, and spices and melt over low/medium heat, stirring frequently until the sugar has dissolved.

2. Increase the heat to bring the mixture to boiling point. Remove from the heat and beat in the baking soda. The mixture will froth up at this point as the baking soda reacts—mix briefly until combined, then let cool for 15 minutes.

3. Sift the flour and salt, then fold into the mixture in batches, using a wooden spoon or a stand mixer. Beat in the egg using a wooden spoon or stand mixer, until just combined. Do not overwork the mixture, or the cookies will spread during baking.

4. The dough will be very sticky to begin with, but do not add any flour. Scrape out of the bowl onto a clean surface and knead together until just smooth. Wrap in plastic wrap and chill in the fridge for 1 hour.

TIP

If using honey in either recipe, then be aware that it can cause your dough to spread a little when baked.

BASICS

ALLERGIES & INTOLERANCES

No one should ever be deprived of baked goods. It is just not fair! Whether you are intolerant or allergic to certain produce, all is not lost. There is a fantastic range of "free from" products available in most large supermarkets or health food stores. They taste great and will allow you to enjoy your sweet treats once again. Simply substitute the "free from" equivalent into the recipes in place of items you must avoid.

Gluten free

Gluten-free flour is usually a blend of rice, potato, tapioca, maize, and buckwheat flours. Making your own is possible, but mixed blends can be bought easily at the supermarket or health food stores. You may find that the dough is a little drier when using gluten-free flour, so add a little extra corn syrup or blackstrap molasses to moisten it.

Dairy free

Dairy-free alternatives to butter, milk, and cream can be easily substituted, such as sunflower spread, coconut oil, soy, almond, hazelnut, or rice milk.

Egg free

With the cookies it is possible just to leave the egg out. The dough is a little crumbly to work with but still manageable—try rolling out between two pieces of parchment paper for best results. The result will be a crisper cookie but it will still taste delicious. You can also substitute with dried egg replacement powder—just follow the package instructions for quantities to substitute per egg. For any egg washes, substitute with oil, milk, or dairy-free milk.

MOLASSES

Molasses is traditionally used in gingerbread as it adds a rich and spicy flavor to baked goods. The term molasses covers any uncrystallized syrups that are a by-product of the sugar-making process. The juice extracted from sugar cane is boiled until some of the sugars crystallize. This juice is then boiled numerous times to extract as much sugar as possible. The thick and sweet syrup that is left is molasses.

The most common types of molasses are the pale syrups known as light molasses and the darker syrups known as dark or blackstrap molasses.

Light molasses

This is the syrup resulting from the first cooking of the sugar cane. Amber in color and similar in appearance to honey, it has the highest sugar content and mildest flavor of the molasses.

Dark molasses

From the second cooking of the sugar cane, dark molasses is slightly thicker and darker in color and has a slightly bitter, richer, and less sweet flavor.

Blackstrap molasses

From the third cooking of the sugar cane, blackstrap molasses is very concentrated and therefore is the darkest, least sweet of all the molasses with a distinctively strong, almost pungent flavor.

I use both light and dark molasses to create two distinguishable colors and strengths of gingerbread. The light dough will give you light golden cookies with a mild, sweet flavor. The dark dough will give you a dark cookie with a stronger, spicier flavor.

The different color doughs can be used to enhance your bakes—so think about how you will decorate your cookies or house when picking your dough recipe, and choose the shade that will compliment it best.

DOUGH TIPS

1. Dough can be made in advance and stored in the fridge allowing time for the spices to permeate the dough. If left for more than a couple of hours in the fridge, you will need to rest the dough at room temperature for 10 to 20 minutes on the side to soften slightly before rolling.

2. Do not over-mix the dough once you have added the egg as it will become quite sticky and difficult to remove from the bowl. Mix it until just combined because this develops the gluten in the dough to make the cookies chewy. Over-mixing will create a tougher end result. However, if it does become sticky, just use a spatula to scrape the dough into a freezer bag and chill as usual.

3. Chilling the dough is an important step. It makes it more pliable and easier to shape.

4. Always chill again in the fridge or freezer after rolling and cutting out the dough. This keeps the cookies from spreading too much and losing their shape.

5. You can use spice mixes such as pumpkin pie spice or Dutch speculaas spice in place of the spices I have included in the recipes. Add up the quantity of individual spices in the recipe and replace the total amount with your spice mix.

6. Using up old spices from the back of the cupboard sounds like a great idea, but on average whole spices only stay fresh for 4 years and ground spices for only 2 years. Buying better quality and fresher spices rather than just what is available at the supermarket will result in a better flavor in your baking. Try specialty whole food stores or ethnic markets where demand is higher so restocking is more frequent. Consider buying whole spices and grinding them yourself so that you can retain maximum flavor and potency. Store your spices away from direct light or heat and keep tightly closed.

7. Using cutters, plastic or metal, will yield a sharper edge and a more uniform batch of cookies than making your own templates and cutting each out. However, sometimes you can't find the right cutter for the job. Then it's best to draw your desired shape onto thick cardstock and cut out using a small, sharp scalpel. Use a new blade or a knife tip to cut out the dough, making sure the dough is well chilled before cutting to keep it from sticking as it takes longer to cut by hand.

BAKING TIPS

1. Longer cooking times will yield stiffer cookies, so if you are constructing a house or something similar that needs support, cook until a little more golden than you might an individual cookie.

2. Use spacers to roll out your dough for perfect, even thickness every time. They can be found in bakeware stores or simple slats of wood cut to size work just as well.

3. Ovens can run hot or cold. I recommend a test bake of a small pan of cookies before baking the whole batch to check the true baking times. Alternatively, buy a small oven thermometer. They are inexpensive and can be a very useful piece of gear for baking.

4. I have used a lower oven temperature to bake my cookies than you might find in other baking books. I found this helped the dough to hold its shape well, and allowed the cookies to cook through entirely without overcooking the surface.

5. For best results, bake a single sheet of cookies in the center of the oven. If baking batches, set racks in the upper and lower thirds of the oven and rotate the pans from top to bottom during baking.

6. The oven temperatures listed in this book are for standard ovens. If you have a fan-assisted or convection oven, simply decrease the temperature by about 35 degrees to achieve the same results.

STORAGE TIPS

1. Humidity is gingerbread's biggest enemy. It affects shelf life and turns gingerbread soft. You should store your gingerbread in a cool, dry environment—preferably in a sealed, airtight container.

2. Gingerbread will keep for up to a month, but longer if kept in an airtight container. If displaying a house or any other bake, keep it out of direct sunlight and display in a cool, dry environment. It will keep for 2 weeks.

3. You can also freeze gingerbread. Wrap the dough in plastic wrap and cover with a plastic bag, then freeze for up to 3 months. Or pack uncooked or cooked gingerbread cookies into containers and freeze for up to 3 to 6 months.

ICING & PIPING

ROYAL ICING

MAKES ABOUT 1½ CUPS

2 cups confectioners'
sugar

1 lightly beaten large
egg white

½ teaspoon
lemon juice

1 teaspoon water

1. Sift the sugar into the bowl of an electric mixer. Add the beaten egg white and lemon juice.

2. Whisk on low speed, so you do not incorporate too much air into the icing, for 2 to 3 minutes until you have a smooth, but not wet, stiff peak consistency. It should be dense and spreadable but hold a stiff peak. If it looks dry and crumbly, add a little water. If it looks slightly runny and glossy, add a little extra confectioners' sugar.

3. You now have stiff peak icing for sticking houses together and placing decorations onto icing. Transfer to a bowl and cover with a damp cloth to prevent it from drying out. The icing can be prepared ahead and stored in an airtight container in the fridge for up to 1 week.

You can adjust this icing to make soft peak and flood icing:

- Soft peak – Add a drop of water at a time until you have icing that holds a soft peak but does not spread on its own. Use for piping lines, borders, and decorations.

- Flood icing – Add a teaspoon of water at a time until you have a thick but runny icing that smooths out on its own within 15 seconds but not so runny that it runs off the edge of your cookie. Use for filling in outlined areas of cookies.

Each recipe will give directions on which type of icing you will need.

TIPS

1. If you have no piping bags, make your own by twisting a tight cone out of parchment paper, or use a small plastic food bag and cut one corner off.

2. If you do not have piping nozzles, you can just cut the end of the piping bag off. Note that a nozzle will give you better results as you have more control.

3. Only half fill the piping bag with icing so it does not ooze out of the top when you squeeze.

4. To make chocolate icing, substitute ¾ cup of cocoa powder in place of an equal amount of confectioners' sugar.

PIPING TIPS

1. Cut the end off your piping bag and insert a small, plain round piping nozzle.

2. Half fill your piping bag with icing, then twist the top of the bag. Secure the end in the hand you are piping with.

3. Touch the starting point with the tip of the piping bag and slowly squeeze out the icing. As you squeeze, lift the bag slightly so you are not dragging it across the cookie—this way you will have a nice, even, smooth line.

4. When you want to finish, bring the bag down to the cookie then stop squeezing and allow the nozzle to touch the cookie at the finishing point to break contact.

CARAMEL GLUE / EDIBLE GLUE

Making caramel isn't for everyone. It can be tricky and during preparation this syrup becomes very hot, so be careful not to burn yourself. If possible, do this part without the kids, or alternatively, use the stiff peak icing on page 14 to stick your house together.

1 cup sugar

¼ cup cold water

TIP

Using a big frying pan for this makes it easy to dip the pieces of gingerbread into the pan to coat the edges.

1. Put the sugar and water in a large, low-sided frying pan. Place over medium-high heat. Without stirring, bring to 320°F on a sugar thermometer. If you do not have one, you will know the syrup is ready when the sugar dissolves and turns a light golden color.

2. Swirl the syrup gently in the pan to even out the color. Then let cool for a few moments to thicken slightly to the consistency of honey.

3. If the syrup begins to harden in the pan, place it back over low heat until it has returned to the required consistency.

COOKIES

A range of cookies to keep a variety
of abilities busy in the kitchen

FESTIVE HANGING COOKIES

MAKES 40 - PREP: 45 MINUTES, PLUS COOLING - COOK: 20 MINUTES

Simply decorated festive cookies add a touch of yum to your tree or home. Perfect for hanging just about anywhere, or to wrap up beautifully and give as a Christmas gift.

1 x quantity of Light or Dark Gingerbread Dough (see page 8)

TO DECORATE

1 x quantity of Royal Icing (see page 14)

red, white, and silver sprinkles

YOU WILL NEED

Christmas cutters

string or ribbon

1. Preheat the oven to 350°F. Line 2 large baking sheets with silicone baking sheets or parchment paper.

2. Cut a large piece of parchment paper and roll out the gingerbread on top of it to ¼ inch. Using any Christmas themed cutter, cut out pieces of dough and use a palette knife to transfer them to the lined baking sheets. Leave space for them to spread a little.

3. Using a straw, press one end into each of the cookies where you would like to thread a ribbon to hang, twist the straw, and pull away to remove a circle of dough. Alternatively, use a skewer to make a hole.

4. Place in the freezer for 5 minutes until hard. Bake in the oven in batches for 6 to 10 minutes depending on size, until golden brown at the edges. Make sure the hanging holes are still large enough to thread ribbon through; if not, use the straw or skewer again to increase the size. Let cool for 5 minutes on the pans, then transfer to wire racks to cool completely.

5. Add a little water to the royal icing until you reach soft peak consistency. Spoon the icing into a piping bag fitted with a fine nozzle. Decorate the cookies with dots, lines, and swirls, then add the sprinkles. Let cool completely for 4 hours before tying with ribbon and hanging.

TIP

Have fun with the hanging materials—use twine, colored ribbon or lace.

GINGERBREAD FAMILY

MAKES 30 - PREP: 40 MINUTES, PLUS COOLING - COOK: 20 MINUTES

There is something very irresistible about gingerbread folk. Their wry little smiles and "catch me if you can" demeanor brings a smile to your face whatever your age. Better still, they keep kids entertained for hours!

1 x quantity of Light Gingerbread Dough (see page 8). Halve the dough once made and add ½ cup of cocoa powder to one half

TO DECORATE

1 x quantity of Royal Icing (see page 14)

colored chocolates

YOU WILL NEED

a set of gingerbread family cutters

1. Preheat the oven to 325°F. Line 2 large baking sheets with silicone baking sheets or parchment paper.

2. Cut a large piece of parchment paper and roll out one of the doughs on top of it to ¼ inch. Using gingerbread men, women, and children cutters, cut out pieces of dough and use a palette knife to transfer them to the lined baking sheets. Leave space for them to spread a little. Repeat with the second gingerbread dough.

3. Place in the freezer for 5 minutes until hard. Bake in the oven in batches for 6 to 10 minutes depending on size, until golden brown at the edges. Let cool for 5 minutes on the pans, then carefully transfer with a palette knife to wire racks to cool completely.

4. Add a little water to the royal icing until you reach a soft peak consistency. Spoon the icing into a piping bag fitted with a fine nozzle. Decorate the gingerbread people with the icing and colored chocolates.

> **TIP** Dip some of the chocolate gingerbread figures in melted chocolate to create chocolate skirts or trousers!

SNOWFLAKE COOKIES

MAKES 45 – PREP: 40 MINUTES, PLUS COOLING – COOK: 20 MINUTES

These sparkling snowflake cookies are perfect for gift giving. Pop them in clear bags or little boxes for anyone who deserves a festive treat.

1 x quantity of Light or Dark Gingerbread Dough (see page 8)

TO DECORATE

2 x quantity of Royal Icing (see page 14)

¼ cup granulated sugar

1 extra-large, free-range egg white

YOU WILL NEED

assorted snowflake cutters approx. 2, 2½, and 3 inches

1. Preheat the oven to 325°F. Line 2 to 3 large baking sheets with silicone baking sheets or parchment paper.

2. Cut a large piece of parchment paper and roll out the gingerbread on top of it to ¼ inch. Using a range of snowflake cutters, cut out cookies and place on the baking sheets. Place larger cookies on one baking sheet and smaller ones on the other so they bake at the same speed.

3. Bake in the oven in batches for 6 to 10 minutes depending on size, until golden brown at the edges. Let cool for 5 minutes on the pans, then transfer to wire racks to cool completely.

4. Add a little water to the royal icing until you reach soft peak consistency. Spoon some of the icing into a piping bag fitted with a fine nozzle. In a steady and smooth line, pipe outlines around half of the snowflakes.

5. Add a little more water to the soft peak icing to make flood icing—a thick but runny consistency. Spoon into a piping bag, cut off the end, and carefully fill the centers with icing. Sprinkle half the sugar over some of the cookies while the icing is still wet.

6. Brush the remaining plain cookies with the egg white and press into the sugar. Let set for 2 hours.

RUDOLPH COOKIES

MAKES 40 – PREP: 1 HOUR 15 MINUTES, PLUS COOLING AND SETTING – COOK: 20 MINUTES

You start with a gingerbread man, turn him upside down, and then you have Rudolph. It is simple and brilliant—the kids will go crazy for these!

1 x quantity of Dark Gingerbread Dough (see page 9)

TO DECORATE

3 x quantity of Royal Icing (see page 14)

red and black food coloring paste

¾ cup cocoa powder

edible gold dust powder

YOU WILL NEED

a gingerbread man cutter approx. 4 inches

1. Preheat the oven to 325°F. Line 2 large baking sheets with silicone baking sheets or parchment paper.

2. Cut a large piece of parchment paper and roll out the gingerbread on top of it to ¼ inch. Using a gingerbread man cutter, cut out pieces of dough and use a palette knife to transfer them to the lined baking sheets.

3. Place in the freezer for 5 minutes until hard. Bake in the oven in batches for 10 minutes until golden brown at the edges. Let cool for 5 minutes then carefully transfer with a palette knife to wire racks to cool completely.

4. Add a little water to the royal icing until you reach soft peak consistency. Get three small bowls and spoon 2 tablespoons of icing into each. Add red coloring to one, black to another, and leave one white. Cover each with a damp cloth and then cover with plastic wrap.

5. Add the cocoa powder to your remaining bowl of icing with a little water to bring it back to soft peak consistency and spoon into a piping bag fitted with a fine nozzle. Pipe outlines of Rudolph's head and antlers. Add a little extra water to the remaining brown icing to make flood icing—a thick but runny consistency. Spoon or pipe into the centers of the cookies to fill the centers with icing. Let set for 4 hours or overnight.

6. For the red noses, repeat the process with the red icing, piping outlines, then filling with the flood icing. Use the white icing to pipe eyes. Let set for 15 minutes then pipe little black pupils and mouths with the black icing. Very carefully, using a paintbrush, dab the gold dust powder and brush gently over the antlers. Let set completely for 1 hour.

GLASS-PRESSED
SANDWICH COOKIES

MAKES 20 · PREP: 30 MINUTES · COOK: 20 MINUTES

This is an inventive way to transform a plain round cookie into something elegant and worthy of serving to friends. It will also have you checking the bottoms of all your kitchenware!

1 x quantity of Light or Dark Gingerbread Dough (see page 8)

14 tablespoons (1 stick + 6 tablespoons) unsalted butter, softened

4 cups confectioners' sugar, sifted

1 teaspoon vanilla extract

pinch of salt

YOU WILL NEED

assorted drinking glasses with embossed bases and a range of round cutters approx. 1½ to 4 inches

TIP

Experiment with anything that would leave a lovely pattern—like rolling the gingerbread dough over paper doilies. Just be sure to chill again before baking so the cookies hold their shape.

1. Preheat the oven to 325°F. Line 2 large baking sheets with silicone baking sheets or parchment paper.

2. Cut a large piece of parchment paper and roll out the gingerbread on top of it to ¼ inch. Now select from your drinking glasses the ones that have the most beautiful patterns on their bases. Press one at a time into the dough firmly enough to leave an imprint but not so hard that you squash the whole cookie! Then use a round cookie cutter approx. 3 inches to cut around the imprinted patterns. Use a range of sizes to make your collection of cookies look more eclectic. Use a palette knife to transfer the cookies onto the lined baking sheets. Leave space for them to spread a little.

3. Place in the freezer for 5 minutes until hard—this second chill helps them to hold their shape and pattern better while baking. Bake in the oven in batches for 8 to 10 minutes until golden brown at the edges. Let cool for 5 minutes on the pans, then carefully transfer with a palette knife to wire racks to cool completely.

4. Beat the butter, confectioners' sugar, vanilla, and salt together with a handheld mixer until light and fluffy. Pipe or spread the butter frosting onto the bases of half the cookies and sandwich together with the remaining cookies.

RUSSIAN DOLLS

MAKES 45 – PREP: 1 HOUR 30 MINUTES, PLUS COOLING AND SETTING – COOK: 20 TO 30 MINUTES

Also known as matryoshka dolls, meaning "little mother," as the dolls inside represent her children. Traditionally these wooden dolls are elaborately painted, so I thought it was fitting to use a paint brush to decorate the cookies.

1 x quantity of Light or Dark Gingerbread Dough (see page 8)

3 x quantity of Royal Icing (see page 14)

TO DECORATE

red, peach, and black food colorings

YOU WILL NEED

Russian doll cutters approx. 2½, 3, and 4 inches

a new fine paintbrush

1. Preheat the oven to 325°F. Line 2 large baking sheets with silicone baking sheets or parchment paper.

2. Cut a large piece of parchment paper and roll out the gingerbread on top of it to ¼ inch. Using Russian doll cutters, cut out pieces of dough and use a palette knife to transfer them to the lined baking sheets.

3. Bake in the oven in batches for 6 to 10 minutes depending on size, until golden brown at the edges. Let cool for 5 minutes on the pans, then transfer to wire racks to cool completely.

4. Add a little water to the royal icing until you reach soft peak consistency. Transfer ¼ cup to a small bowl, then cover the large bowl with a damp cloth and set aside. Add a little peach coloring to the icing and pipe small round circles for the doll faces. Add a little extra water to the remaining peach icing to make flood icing—a think but runny consistency. Spoon into the circles to fill the faces.

5. Transfer 2 tablespoons of the remaining white icing to a separate bowl, cover with a damp cloth, and set aside. Add a little red food coloring to the large bowl of icing until you have a punchy red. With a fine nozzle, pipe a smooth red outline around the cookies.

6. Add a little more water to the red icing to make flood icing, then use it to carefully fill the centers. Keep any remaining icing covered with a damp cloth. Let set completely for 4 hours or overnight.

7. Using a paintbrush and the reserved white icing, paint decorative patterns on the dolls' bodies and around the faces. Paint little red lips on the faces and tiny dots for nostrils. Use a drop of black coloring to paint eyes and eyelashes. Leave one final time to set for 2 hours.

TIP

Many snowman cutters have a very similar shape to a Russian doll, so check your cutter stash before buying a new one.

SPECULAAS

MAKES 12 LARGE COOKIES · PREP: 40 MINUTES, PLUS CHILLING · COOK: 10 TO 15 MINUTES

I grew up eating these, quite stale funnily enough, as they are baked in the Netherlands to celebrate Sinterklass/St. Nicolas Eve on December 5th, but at Easter my sisters and I would visit my great Oma (Dutch for grandma) and she would give them to us!

7 tablespoons butter, softened

⅔ cup light brown sugar

1 large free-range egg

zest of 1 lemon

1⅔ cups all-purpose flour, plus extra to dust the molds

½ teaspoon baking powder

1 teaspoon ground cinnamon

1 teaspoon ground ginger

¼ teaspoon ground nutmeg

¼ teaspoon ground cloves

⅛ teaspoon ground white pepper

2 cardamom pods, husks removed and seeds ground

¼ teaspoon salt

½ cup ground almonds

¼ cup flaked almonds

1 tablespoon milk

YOU WILL NEED

a speculaas plank—a wooden mold with an image or figure approx. 4 x 3 x ¼ inch You can buy them in cookware shops, antique shops, or online.

1. Put the butter and sugar in a large bowl and beat with an electric mixer until light and fluffy. Beat in the egg and lemon zest until well combined. Sift in the flour, baking powder, spices, and salt and fold in with the ground almonds. Bring the dough together with your hands. Split into 2 balls, wrap in plastic wrap, and chill in the fridge for 1 hour.

2. Preheat the oven to 325°F. Line 2 large baking sheets with silicone baking sheets or parchment paper. Take one half of the dough out of the fridge, keeping the other dough chilled, because if it becomes sticky it is difficult to remove from the molds.

3. Sprinkle a generous amount of flour into the speculaas plank, then brush excess gently out with a pastry brush. Take a small handful of dough and press into the mold. Use a sharp knife to cut away any excess. Press a few flaked almonds into the underside of the cookies then tap gently out of the molds. If they need a little help, run the tip of a knife around the edges. Check the mold frequently and clear away any dough left behind with a skewer.

4. Place on the lined baking sheets and repeat with the remaining dough. Chill the cookies in the freezer for 20 minutes. This second chill helps them to hold their shape better while baking.

5. Brush lightly with milk and bake in the oven for 10 to 15 minutes, until just golden brown at the edges. Let cool for 5 minutes on the pans, then transfer to wire racks to cool completely.

TIP If you do not have a speculaas plank, use a cookie cutter or imprint with nice glass bases as on page 28.

GINGERBREAD SPICED
SPRINGERLE

MAKES 12 COOKIES - PREP: 45 MINUTES, PLUS CHILLING AND SETTING - COOK: 10 TO 15 MINUTES

Originating from Germany, these cookies are made with hand-carved wooden molds. You can pick up gorgeous molds or rolling pins from antique stores. You can also use the imprinting method on page 33 used for the Speculaas cookies.

¼ teaspoon baking powder

2 tablespoons milk

3 medium free-range eggs

3 cups confectioners' sugar

5 tablespoons unsalted butter, softened

zest of 1 lemon

1 teaspoon ground ginger

½ teaspoon ground cinnamon

¼ teaspoon ground nutmeg

¼ teaspoon ground cloves

½ teaspoon salt

3½ cups all-purpose flour, plus extra for dusting

YOU WILL NEED

a Springerle mold, approx. 4½-inch diameter x ½-inch deep

1. Line 2 large baking sheets with silicone baking sheets or parchment paper. Stir the baking powder into 1 tablespoon of the milk and set aside for 30 minutes until dissolved.

2. Place the eggs in the bowl of a stand mixer and whisk on high speed for 10 minutes until thick and pale. Slowly add the confectioners' sugar, beating until creamy. Add the butter, zest, spices, and salt and beat again until smooth and combined. Add the dissolved baking powder and milk and mix until just combined. On a slow speed, gradually add the flour in batches until the beater can't blend any more. Turn onto a clean surface and knead in more flour to make a stiff dough. Wrap in plastic wrap and chill in the fridge for 20 minutes.

3. Dust the surface with flour and roll out the gingerbread to ½ inch. Sprinkle a generous amount of flour into the springerle mold. Gently brush excess out with a pastry brush. Imprint the dough with your mold, and cut around the mold with a sharp knife or use a cookie cutter of a similar size. Press, cut, and transfer to the lined baking sheets one at a time, so when you press the next one it does not distort the first. Leave to air-dry, uncovered, for 24 hours—this helps to preserve the detail of the surface pattern.

4. Preheat the oven to 325°F. Lightly brush with the remaining milk and bake in the oven for 10 to 15 minutes depending on size, until lightly golden. Let cool for 5 minutes on the pans, then transfer to wire racks to cool completely.

HOUSES

They look too good to eat,
but smell too good not to!

TOWN HOUSE

MAKES 1 HOUSE - PREP: 3 HOURS - COOK: 1 HOUR 15 MINUTES

This London town house will be your chic alternative to a traditional gingerbread house.

2 x quantity of Light or Dark Gingerbread Dough (see page 8)

1 x quantity of Caramel Glue (see page 16)

TO DECORATE

2 x quantity of Royal Icing (see page 14)

2 to 3 large sheets rice paper

YOU WILL NEED

the templates on page 96

TIP

You might find it easier to use some of the royal icing to help stick tricky parts together rather than using the glue.

1. See the templates on page 96. Using a ruler, cut out firm paper or cardstock versions. Preheat the oven to 325°F. Cut a large piece of parchment paper and roll out the gingerbread on top of it to ¼ inch. Using the templates, cut out the pieces.

2. Transfer on the parchment paper to a baking sheet. Place in the freezer for 10 minutes until hard. Bake in the oven in batches for 10 to 20 minutes, depending on size, until golden brown at the edges (see tip on page 48). Let cool for 5 minutes on the pans, then transfer to wire racks to cool completely.

3. Add a little water to the royal icing until you reach soft peak consistency. Spoon into a piping bag fitted with a fine nozzle. Cut the rice paper ½ to ¾ inch larger than the grid of windows. Pipe around and between the windows on the underside of the gingerbread and stick the trimmed rice paper into place. Repeat for the roof windows. Pipe around the front door and attach the door piece so the door sits back from the front of the house. Pipe the window frames and panes.

4. Stick the lower fascia detail to the front and back using a little icing or glue. Then pipe around the outside of the lower third and around the windows. Save a little icing for sticking but add a little water to the remaining to make flood icing. Fill the piped areas until covered. Let set for 4 hours or overnight.

5. To assemble, dip one edge of the side wall into the caramel glue until the edge is covered. Attach to a front at a 90° angle and hold together while it hardens and sets. Continue by attaching another wall and then the back. Use a pastry brush to coat the top edges and attach the main roof. Stick on the remaining fascia details. Attach the roof windows to the walls, stick the top with the roof, then add the chimney pieces. Pipe 2 lines around the tops of the chimneys. Let set for 2 hours, then place on the base of the house.

HOLLY ROOF HOUSE

MAKES 1 HOUSE - PREP: 2 HOURS, PLUS COOLING & SETTING - COOK: 1 HOUR

If you want a Christmas showstopper, look no further. Far from the overly decorated gingerbread houses full of sweets, this one is for the adults. It's glamorous and tempting—let's just hope you get to show it off before you break and eat it!

2 x quantity of Light or Dark Gingerbread Dough (see page 8)

1 x quantity of Caramel Glue (see page 16)

TO DECORATE

3 x quantity of Royal Icing (see page 14)

red and green food coloring paste

YOU WILL NEED

the templates on page 98

ribbon

1. See the templates on page 98. Using a ruler, cut out firm paper or cardstock versions. Preheat the oven to 325°F. Cut a large piece of parchment paper and roll out the gingerbread on top of it to ¼ inch. Using the templates, cut out the house pieces. You can use any leftover dough to make gingerbread men.

2. Cut three thick slits on each of the roofs (see image on page 42) for the ribbon to hold the roof up. Transfer carefully on the parchment paper to a flat baking sheet. Keep the dough on the parchment paper to prevent it from becoming misshapen while you move it. Place in the freezer for 10 minutes until hard then bake in the oven in batches for 10 to 20 minutes depending on size, until golden brown at the edges (see tip on page 48). Let cool for 5 minutes on the pans, then transfer to wire racks to cool completely.

3. To glue together, dip one edge of a front wall into the caramel glue until the edge is completely covered. Attach to a side wall at a 90° angle and hold together for a few moments while it hardens, then use cans or jars to support the walls while they set. Continue to stick together by attaching another wall and the back panel so you have the base of the gingerbread house. Let set completely for 1 hour or overnight. It needs to be firm to hold the weight of the roof.

4. Meanwhile, add a little water to the royal icing until you reach soft peak consistency. Spoon some of the icing into a piping bag fitted with a medium nozzle. Decorate by piping outlines of windows and doors, etc.

5. Lay the roof pieces flat and in a steady and smooth line, pipe outlines around the edges. Add a little extra water to two thirds of the soft peak icing to make flood icing—a thick but runny consistency. Spoon into a piping bag, cut off the end, and carefully fill the centers with icing. Let set for 4 hours or overnight.

6. Once completely set, divide the remaining soft peak icing into two bowls and add a little red coloring paste to one and green to the other. Spoon into piping bags fitted with a fine nozzle to pipe holly leaves and berries and use a toothpick to drag out edges of the holly leaves. Add a little green icing or coloring paste to the leftover red icing to make it brown and pipe the holly tree branches. Carefully thread the roof panels with some ribbon and tie up together.

7. Remove the supports from the house and gently place the roof on the house.

HANSEL & GRETEL HOUSE

MAKES 1 HOUSE - PREP: 2 HOURS, PLUS COOLING & SETTING - COOK: 1 HOUR

Gingerbread houses are intricately linked to the Brothers Grimm fairy tale of *Hansel and Gretel* about a brother and sister who become lost in a forest and, when hungry and tired, they stumble across a house constructed of gingerbread and sweets! For most, this would be a dream come true!

2 x quantity of Light or Dark Gingerbread Dough (see page 8)

1 x quantity of Caramel Glue (see page 16)

TO DECORATE

1 x quantity of Royal Icing (see page 14)

mini candy canes

lots of colorful sweets and chocolates

YOU WILL NEED

the templates on page 102

1. See the templates on page 102. Using a ruler, cut out firm paper or cardstock versions. Preheat the oven to 325°F. Cut a large piece of parchment paper and roll out the gingerbread on top of it to ¼ inch.

2. Using the templates, cut out the house pieces. Transfer carefully on the parchment paper to a flat baking sheet. Keep the dough on the parchment paper to prevent it from becoming misshapen while you move it.

3. You can also cut a door or windows if you wish; it is best to do this once the dough is on the baking sheet—again this is to avoid misshaping it. Place in the freezer for 10 minutes until hard, then bake in the oven in batches for 10 to 20 minutes depending on size, until golden brown at the edges (see tip on page 48). Let cool for 5 minutes on the pans, then transfer to wire racks to cool completely.

4. To glue together, dip one edge of a front wall into the caramel glue until the edge is completely covered. Attach to a side wall at a 90° angle and hold together for a few moments while it hardens and sets. Use cans or jars at first to support the walls while they set. Continue to stick together by attaching another wall and the back panel so you have the base of the gingerbread house. Let set completely for 30 minutes.

5. Remove the supports from the house and fix the roof panels on. You will need to reheat the caramel glue to return it to a liquid state. Use a pastry brush to coat the edges of the roof panels and edges of the base of the house where you will stick them. As the angle

is steep, you will need to hold these on firmly for a few minutes while they begin to set. Let set for 30 minutes.

6. Add a little water to the royal icing until you reach soft peak consistency. Spoon the icing into a piping bag fitted with a fine nozzle. Decorate by piping outlines of windows and doors, elaborate scalloped patterns on the roof, etc. Stick many colorful sweets to your house so that it really is too good to eat!

> **TIP** Never throw away scraps of gingerbread—use them to make trees or gingerbread men to place beside your house.

GINGERBREAD STREET

MAKES 3 HOUSES - PREP: 2 HOURS, PLUS COOLING & SETTING - COOK: 1 HOUR

This street makes a lovely Christmas centerpiece when you cut out doors and windows and have candles or fairy lights twinkling around them.

2 x quantity of Light or Dark Gingerbread dough (see page 8)

TO DECORATE

3 x quantity of Royal Icing (see page 14)

licorice wheel or edible sweet laces

1 x quantity of Caramel Glue (see page 16), optional

colorful chocolate candies or sweets

YOU WILL NEED

the templates on pages 99 to 101

TIP

Bake gingerbread for houses a little longer than individual cookies as longer cooking times yield stiffer cookies.

1. See the templates on pages 99 to 101. Using a ruler, cut out firm paper or cardstock versions. Preheat the oven to 325°F. Cut a large piece of parchment paper and roll out the gingerbread on top of it to ¼ inch.

2. Using the templates, cut out the house pieces and carefully transfer on the parchment paper (to prevent it from becoming misshapen while you move it) to a baking sheet.

3. Place in the freezer for 5 minutes until hard, then bake in the oven in batches for 6 to 12 minutes depending on size, until golden brown at the edges. Let cool for 5 minutes, then transfer to wire racks to cool completely.

4. Add a little water to the royal icing until you reach soft peak consistency. Spoon one third of the icing into a piping bag fitted with a fine nozzle. To assemble the houses, pipe along the side edges of the wall pieces and stick to the front and back pieces. Pipe extra icing where the walls join each other on the inside of the house to create some support. Pipe icing onto the top edges of the side panels and front/back pieces where the roof pieces will be placed. Stick on the roofs and hold for a minute until the icing starts to set. Pipe decorations onto the houses.

5. Unroll the licorice. Using icing or caramel glue, stick the colorful sweets to the licorice and let set. Once set, stick to the front edge of the houses to look like festive street lights.

6. Add a little extra water to the remaining icing to make flood icing—a thick but runny consistency. Spoon over the peaks of the roofs and allow to drip down the sides. Let set for 2 hours or overnight.

COUNTRY COTTAGE

MAKES 1 HOUSE – PREP: 2 HOURS, PLUS COOLING & SETTING – COOK: 1 HOUR

An enchanting country cottage, complete with a porch and stained glass windows. Decorate simply with your favorite colors and interesting shapes!

2 x quantity of Light or Dark Gingerbread Dough (see page 8)

1 x quantity of Caramel Glue (see page 16)

TO DECORATE

2 x quantity of Royal Icing (see page 14)

7 ounces hard yellow candy, melted

1¾ ounces mints

YOU WILL NEED

the templates on pages 103 to 106

a 1½-inch heart cutter

1. See the templates on pages 103 to 106. Using a ruler, cut out firm paper or cardstock versions. Preheat the oven to 325°F. Cut a large piece of parchment paper and roll out the gingerbread on top of it to ¼ inch.

2. Using the templates, cut out the house pieces, then cut out the door and windows. Carefully transfer on the parchment paper (to prevent it from becoming misshapen while you move it) to a flat baking sheet.

3. Using a 1½-inch heart cutter, cut a window on the front panel of the porch and above the windows on the side panels. Crush half the boiled sweets to a powder. Pile high in the window and heart holes.

4. Add the hearts you have cut out to a baking sheet. Place all the dough in the freezer for 10 minutes until hard, then bake in the oven in batches for 8 to 15 minutes depending on size, until golden brown at the edges (see tip on page 48). Let cool for 5 minutes on the pans, then transfer to wire racks to cool completely.

5. To glue together, dip one edge of a front wall into the caramel glue until the edge is completely covered. Attach to a side wall at a 90° angle and hold together for a few moments while it hardens and sets. Continue to stick together by attaching another wall and the back panel so you have the base of the gingerbread house. Use cans or jars to support the walls while they set. Stick the porch base together and stick to the house. Let set completely for 30 minutes.

6. Remove the supports from the house and fix the roof panels on using a pastry brush to coat the edges of the roof panels and edges of the base of the house where you will stick them. Then attach the roof panels to the porch. Use the caramel glue to stick the chimney pieces together. Once hard, glue to the roof.

7. Add a little water to the royal icing until you reach soft peak consistency. Spoon some of the icing into a piping bag fitted with a fine nozzle. Decorate by piping scalloped lines onto the roof for a tiled roof, snow onto the window frames, and outline the door. Finish by using the soft peak icing to stick colored sweets to your house.

CREATIONS

From a chocolate bird house to a hanging
wreath, there are plenty of ideas here
to inspire your next edible project

EDIBLE STAR WREATH

MAKES 1 WREATH - PREP: 2 HOURS, PLUS CHILLING & SETTING - COOK: 45 MINUTES

Bake this pretty wreath to hang on your door or serve it as a fun, sharing dessert!

2 x quantity of Light or Dark Gingerbread Dough (see page 8)

2 x quantity of Royal Icing (see page 14)

1 x quantity of Caramel Glue (see page 16)

TO DECORATE

blue food coloring paste

silver balls

YOU WILL NEED

star cutters approx. 1¼, 2, and 3 inches

1. Preheat the oven to 325°F. Line 3 large baking sheets with silicone baking sheets or parchment paper.

2. Cut a large piece of parchment paper and roll out the gingerbread on top of it to ¼ inch. Place a 10-inch plate on the dough and cut around it. Then use a smaller plate or bowl to cut out the center—you want a ring 1½ inches wide.

3. Using different-sized star cutters, cut out shapes from the remaining dough. You will need about 30 cookies. Place in the freezer for 5 minutes until hard. Bake in the oven in batches for 6 to 15 minutes depending on size, until golden brown at the edges. Bake the wreath ring for 15 minutes or until golden as it will need to be sturdy. Let cool for 5 minutes on the pans, then carefully transfer with a palette knife to wire racks to cool completely.

4. Add a little water to the royal icing until you reach soft peak consistency. Divide between 2 bowls and color one with blue coloring paste. Spoon each into piping bags fitted with fine nozzles. Pipe outlines around half the snowflakes. Pipe decorations onto the plain stars.

5. Squeeze two thirds of the icing out of the piping bags into separate bowls and add water to make flood icing—a thick but runny consistency. Spoon into the cookies lined with the same color. Stud a few with silver balls. Let set for 2 hours, then use the remaining soft peak icing to pipe more detail onto the stars.

6. Arrange the largest stars on the ring. Once you are happy with the placing, brush the backs of the stars with caramel glue and stick to the circle. Repeat with the remaining stars. Let set. Hang with a ribbon.

MINI MUG GINGERBREAD HOUSES

MAKES 15 HOUSES - PREP: 1 HOUR 30 MINUTES, PLUS CHILLING & COOLING - COOK: 20 MINUTES

These mini houses sit happily on the edge of your mug and go perfectly with an afternoon cup of tea. Or try them with a gingerbread latte using the syrup on page 94.

1 x quantity of Light Gingerbread Dough (see page 8)

TO DECORATE

2 x quantity of Royal Icing (see page 14)

confectioners' sugar, to dust

white sprinkles and snowflakes

YOU WILL NEED

the templates on page 107

1. Preheat the oven to 325°F. Line 2 or 3 large baking sheets with silicone baking sheets or parchment paper. See the templates on page 107. Using a ruler, cut out firm paper or cardstock versions.

2. Cut a large piece of parchment paper and roll out the gingerbread on top of it to ¼ inch. Using the templates, cut out the house pieces. Place on a lined baking sheet. Repeat to make 14 more houses.

3. Place in the freezer for 5 minutes until hard. Bake in the oven for 5 to 6 minutes or until golden brown at the edges. Use the flat edge of a sharp knife to straighten any edges that have spread during baking, especially the doorway so it will fit over the rim of your mugs. Let cool for 5 minutes on the pans, then transfer with a palette knife to wire racks to cool.

4. Add a little water to the royal icing until you reach soft peak consistency. Spoon some of the icing into a piping bag fitted with a fine nozzle. Pipe along the side edges of the wall pieces and stick to the door pieces. Pipe extra icing where the walls join each other on the inside of the house to create some support.

5. Pipe icing onto the top edges of the side panels and front/back pieces where the roof pieces will be placed. Stick on the roofs and hold for a minute until the icing starts to set, then stick on the chimneys.

6. Use the remaining icing to decorate. Cover some of the roofs with icing and sprinkle with decorations. Use a toothpick to help create icicles. Let set for 2 hours or overnight.

TIP

Check the thickness of your mugs. Usually they are ⅛ inch, but if you think yours are thicker, make the door opening a little wider.

CHRISTMAS COOKIE TREE

MAKES 1 LARGE TREE - PREP: 1 HOUR 30 MINUTES, PLUS CHILLING & SETTING - COOK: 1 HOUR

This cookie tree is so simple yet it looks so impressive (even if the kids help to make it!). A little dusting of confectioners' sugar or sprinkles add to the magic.

1 x quantity of Light or Dark Gingerbread Dough (see page 8)

TO DECORATE

2 x quantity of Royal Icing (see page 14)

2 tablespoons confectioners' sugar

sprinkles, optional

1. Preheat the oven to 325°F. Line 2 or 3 large baking sheets with silicone baking sheets or parchment paper. Using a ruler, draw and cut out an 8-inch star onto firm paper or cardstock. Then inside this star draw smaller stars decreasing by ¾ inch each time, your last star being ¾ inch.

2. Cut a large piece of parchment paper and roll out the gingerbread on top of it to ¼ inch. Cut out three of the largest stars and, using a palette knife, transfer to the lined baking sheets. Place in the freezer for 5 minutes until hard, then bake in the oven in batches for 6 to 10 minutes depending on size, until golden brown at the edges. Let cool for 5 minutes on the pans, then carefully transfer with a palette knife to wire racks to cool completely.

3. Trim the star template to the next size and cut out three dough stars, chill, and bake as above decreasing the bake time to 6 to 8 minutes for medium stars and to 3 to 6 minutes for the small stars. Keep repeating until you have baked three of each star.

4. Add a little water to the royal icing until you reach soft peak consistency. Spoon into a piping bag fitted with a medium round nozzle and pipe around each of the stars. Add a little more water to the remaining icing to make flood icing, and spoon or pipe into the lines of each cookie spreading to the edges. Let set for 30 minutes, then stack the stars up starting with the largest and ending with the smallest on its edge. Dust with the confectioners' sugar and decorate with sprinkles if you wish.

TIP

I like to make one giant tree that slowly gets devoured, but you could make a few smaller trees to display together or enjoy at different times.

CHOCOLATE BIRD HOUSE

MAKES 1 HOUSE PLUS 20 BIRDS - PREP: 2 HOURS, PLUS COOLING & SETTING - COOK: 1 HOUR

For the more whimsical among you, this is the perfect project. It is also a great excuse to make a gingerbread house at any time of the year!

1 x quantity of Dark Gingerbread Dough (see page 9). Add ¾ cup of cocoa to the dough to make it chocolate flavored

1 x quantity of Caramel Glue (see page 16)

TO DECORATE

2 x quantity of Royal Icing (see page 14)

blue, yellow, and black food coloring paste

5½ ounces dark chocolate, melted

9 ounces large chocolate buttons

3½ ounces chocolate Matchmakers/sticks

YOU WILL NEED

the templates on page 108

1. See the templates on page 108. Using a ruler, cut out firm paper or cardstock versions. Preheat the oven to 325°F. Cut a large piece of parchment paper and roll out the gingerbread on top of it to ¼ inch. Using the templates, cut out the house pieces.

2. Transfer carefully on the parchment paper (to prevent it from becoming misshapen while you move it) to a flat baking sheet. Place in the freezer for 5 minutes until hard, then bake in the oven in batches for 10 to 15 minutes depending on size, until golden brown at the edges. Let cool for 5 minutes on the pans, then transfer to wire racks to cool completely.

3. Using bird cutters, cut out pieces from the remaining dough and bake for 8 minutes. Let cool for 5 minutes on the pans, then transfer to wire racks to cool completely.

4. To assemble the house, dip one edge of the front wall into the caramel glue until the edge is completely covered. Attach to a side wall at a 90° angle and hold together for a few moments while it hardens and sets. Continue to stick together by attaching another wall and the back panel so you have the base of the bird house. To fix the roof panels on, you may need to reheat the caramel glue to return it to a liquid state. Use a pastry brush to coat the edges of the roof panels and edges of the base of the house where you will stick them. Hold these on firmly for a few minutes while they begin to set. Let set for 30 minutes.

5. Meanwhile, add a little water to the royal icing until you reach soft peak consistency. Spoon one third into a bowl, cover with a damp cloth, and set aside. In the large bowl of icing, stir through a little blue coloring paste, spoon half into a piping bag fitted with a fine nozzle, and pipe an outline around the birds. Add a little extra water to the remaining blue icing to make flood icing—a thick but runny consistency. Spoon or pipe into the centers of the cookies. Let set completely, about 2 hours.

6. Add yellow food coloring to the reserved icing and use to pipe wing details and beaks. Use a paintbrush and black coloring mixed with a drop of water to draw eyes and feet. Let set for 1 hour.

7. Sit the bird house on the round base. Brush the bottom 1¼ inch of the roof with melted chocolate and cover with a row of chocolate buttons. Repeat brushing and sticking rows up the roof to the top. Repeat the process with the front but with chocolate sticks, breaking pieces to fit flush with the edges.

8. Use a small blob of chocolate to stick a couple of birds in place. I like to keep the remaining bird cookies stacked up in the bird house!

GINGERBREAD GARLAND

MAKES 4 GARLANDS - PREP: 40 MINUTES - COOK: 20 MINUTES

This adorable gingerbread garland is a great activity for the kids in the run up to Christmas. Just make sure you hang it out of the reach of young children or pets... or the cookies will be enjoyed before you get a chance!

1 x quantity of Light Gingerbread Dough (see page 8). Halve the dough once made and add ½ cup of cocoa powder to one half

YOU WILL NEED
gingerbread man and heart cutters approx. 2¼ inches

4 x 3-foot lengths of ribbon

TIP

Hang against a flat surface to prevent the weight from rolling the cookies forward.

1. Preheat the oven to 325°F. Line 2 large baking sheets with silicone baking sheets or parchment paper. Cut a large piece of parchment paper and roll out the gingerbread on top of it to ¼ inch.

2. Using a gingerbread man and heart cutter, cut out pieces of dough and use a palette knife to transfer them to the lined baking sheets. Leave space for them to spread a little. Repeat with the other dough. Place in the freezer for 5 minutes until hard.

3. Cut two slits in the center of each cookie ½ inch apart, large enough to thread a ribbon through. Bake in the oven in batches for 12 minutes, until golden brown at the edges. Check that the slits are still large enough, if not cut back to size. Let cool for 5 minutes on the pans, then carefully transfer with a palette knife to wire racks to cool completely.

4. Thread the cookies onto a long piece of ribbon, always starting at the back of the cookie going through to the front, then turning and threading back through to the back. This ensures that the length of the ribbon always stays at the back of the garland, so it doesn't cover the cookies. Don't pull the ribbon too tight when hanging or the pressure will break the center of the cookies.

WILDLIFE WONDERLAND

MAKES 1 LARGE TREE & 20 ASSORTED ANIMALS - PREP: 1 HOUR, PLUS 30 MINUTES CHILLING - COOK: 50 MINUTES

Bring your cookies to life by adding a little stand and surrounding them with edible earth and trees!

2 x quantity of Light or Dark Gingerbread Dough (see page 8)

1 x quantity of Caramel Glue (see page 16)

TO DECORATE

7 ounces white chocolate, melted

½ cup mixed green and white sprinkles

2 x quantity of Royal Icing (see page 14)

¾ cup cocoa powder

3 cups cookie crumbs

1. Preheat the oven to 325°F. Line 2 or 3 large baking sheets with silicone baking sheets or parchment paper. Cut a large piece of parchment paper and roll out the gingerbread on top of it to ¼ inch.

2. Using any wildlife themed cutter, cut out pieces of dough and use a palette knife to transfer them to lined baking sheets. Leave space for them to spread a little. If you want to stand your cookies, use a small round cookie cutter to cut pieces of dough large enough to stand your wildlife cookies on. Place in the freezer for 5 minutes until hard, then bake in the oven in batches for 6 to 10 minutes depending on size, until golden brown at the edges. Let cool for 5 minutes on the pans, then carefully transfer with a palette knife to wire racks to cool completely.

3. Make a large 3D tree following the method on page 72 for the 3D Christmas tree cookies. But instead of making lots of little trees, make one large one. If you do not have a large cutter, make a template for a large tree out of cardstock. Chill, bake, and cool as above.

4. Once cool, use a pastry brush to brush the white chocolate down the edges of the tree and scatter with or press into the sprinkles. Let set before slotting the three cookies into each other.

5. Add a little water to the royal icing until you reach soft peak consistency. Spoon half into a piping bag fitted with a small round nozzle. Stir the cocoa powder into the remaining icing, adding a little water to return it to soft peak. Spoon into a separate piping bag fitted with a small round nozzle. Use both icings to pipe details onto the animals. Let set completely for 2 hours.

6. Spoon a little caramel glue onto the cookie bases, place the animal cookies on the glue, and hold for a moment while they begin to set. Scatter the cookie crumbs over a board and arrange the wildlife around the tree.

3D CHRISTMAS TREE

MAKES 18 · PREP: 2 HOURS, PLUS COOLING & SETTING · COOK: 20 TO 30 MINUTES

These fun trees stand up by themselves and make for a much more exciting Christmas tree cookie! You can use this recipe to make small trees for individual servings, large trees for sharing, or to display beside a gingerbread house.

1 x quantity of Light or Dark Gingerbread Dough (see page 8)

TO DECORATE

7 ounces white chocolate, melted

½ cup mixed green and white sprinkles

YOU WILL NEED

a tree cutter approx. 4 inches

the template on page 109

1. Take your tree cutter and trace three times onto thick cardstock. Using a ruler, draw a vertical line straight down the center of the trees. Draw two more lines ½ inch on either side of your first line. Cut around the trees, cutting off the tree trunk to make it more stable.

2. Refer to page 109 for how to cut your tree templates. Measure from the top of the tree to the bottom and divide by three. Double this measurement, add ¼ inch, and mark on your first tree measuring from the bottom up. For the second tree, use your original measurement, add ¼ inch, and mark from the top down and then the bottom up. For the third, double the original measurement, add ¼ inch, and measure from the top down. Cut down the two widest lines to your marks and remove to create slots.

3. Preheat the oven to 325°F. Line 2 large baking sheets with silicone baking sheets or parchment paper. Cut a large piece of parchment paper and roll out the gingerbread on top of it to ¼ inch.

4. Using your tree cutter, cut out pieces of dough three at a time for each cookie. Transfer to the lined baking sheets. Using the templates and a sharp knife, cut out the slots and remove the trunk from each cookie. Repeat with the remaining dough.

5. Place in the freezer for 5 minutes until hard. Bake in the oven in batches for 8 to 10 minutes, until golden at the edges. Let cool for 5 minutes, then transfer with a palette knife to wire racks to cool completely.

6. Using a pastry brush, brush the white chocolate down the edges of the trees and scatter with the sprinkles. Let set before slotting the 3 cookies into each other.

BAKED TREATS

For when you crave something
a little softer and stickier

GINGERBREAD LAYER CAKE
WITH MAPLE FROSTING

SERVES: 12 - PREP: 40 MINUTES - COOK: 30 TO 35 MINUTES

A great alternative to Christmas cake that is rich and sticky with a tangy cream cheese frosting. Decorate with Mini Gingerbread Houses for a show stopper!

⅓ cup dark or blackstrap molasses

⅓ cup corn syrup or honey

1 cup light brown sugar

17 tablespoons (2 sticks + 1 tablespoon) softened butter

3 large free-range eggs

1 cup milk

2¾ cups all-purpose flour

1½ teaspoons baking soda

2 teaspoons ground ginger

1 teaspoon cinnamon

1 teaspoon allspice

¼ teaspoon nutmeg

½ teaspoon salt

zest of 1 lemon

TO DECORATE

17 tablespoons (2 sticks + 1 tablespoon) softened butter

4 cups confectioners' sugar

9 ounces full-fat cream cheese at room temperature

2 tablespoons maple syrup

3 tablespoons dried coconut flakes

2 x Mini Gingerbread Mug Houses (see page 60)

YOU WILL NEED

3 x 7-inch round cake pans

1. Preheat the oven to 325°F. Grease and line the cake pans with parchment paper.

2. Pour the molasses, syrup, sugar, and butter into a large saucepan and melt over low/medium heat, stirring frequently until the sugar has dissolved. Pour into the bowl of a stand mixer or a large bowl and let cool for 10 minutes.

3. Beat the eggs and milk together, then beat into the cooled molasses mixture with a handheld or stand mixer. Sift the remaining dry ingredients over the wet mix and beat in with the lemon zest until just combined.

4. Divide the batter evenly between the lined pans. Bake in the oven for 20 to 25 minutes, until risen and a skewer emerges clean. Let cool for 10 minutes in the pans, then transfer to wire racks to cool completely.

5. Using a stand mixer or electric hand mixer, beat the butter and confectioners' sugar together until pale and fluffy. Add the cream cheese and continue to beat for another 2 minutes until smooth, then beat in the maple syrup for another 30 seconds.

6. Spread a little frosting over the first layer of cake, then top with the next layer of cake. Repeat once more, then use the remaining frosting to top the cake and cover the sides. Sprinkle with the coconut and top with Mini Gingerbread Houses.

GINGERBREAD CUPCAKES
WITH CHOCOLATE FROSTING

MAKES 12 – PREP:40 MINUTES, PLUS COOLING – COOK: 30 MINUTES

Sticky dark English gingerbread cupcakes smothered in chocolate buttercream. Use up leftover gingerbread dough to make mini gingerbread man cookies to decorate.

10 tablespoons unsalted butter, softened

1 cup dark brown sugar

½ cup dark or blackstrap molasses

zest of 1 orange

1 teaspoon ground cinnamon

1 teaspoon ground ginger

½ teaspoon ground nutmeg

¼ teaspoon ground allspice

3 large free-range eggs

½ cup applesauce

1¼ cups all-purpose flour

½ teaspoon baking powder

½ teaspoon baking soda

¼ teaspoon salt

FROSTING AND DECORATION

17 tablespoons (2 sticks + 1 tablespoon) butter, softened

2½ cups confectioners' sugar, sifted

3½ ounces dark chocolate, melted and cooled

1 ounce crystallized ginger or mini gingerbread men (see page 22)

1. Preheat the oven to 325°F. Line a 12-hole muffin pan with cupcake liners.

2. Put the butter, sugar, molasses, zest, and spices in a medium saucepan and melt over low/medium heat. Stir frequently until the sugar has dissolved. Pour into the bowl of a stand mixer or a large bowl and let cool for 10 minutes.

3. Add the eggs one at a time, beating well with a handheld or stand mixer after each addition. Beat in the applesauce. Sift in the dry ingredients, then mix on a slow speed until just combined.

4. Spoon the mixture into the cupcake liners. Use a large ice cream scoop to make the cakes even sizes. Bake in the oven for 20 minutes, until risen and a skewer emerges clean. Let cool for 10 minutes in the muffin pan, then transfer to wire racks to cool completely.

5. Beat the butter and confectioners' sugar together with a handheld mixer until light and fluffy. Add the cooled chocolate and beat until smooth and combined. Spoon into a piping bag fitted with a large open star nozzle.

6. Hold the bag vertically and pipe in a spiral pattern, working from the outside edge inward, keeping a constant pressure on the piping bag. Continue in a spiral motion, creating another layer of frosting, working gradually toward the center. To finish, release the pressure on the bag, press down lightly, then draw up sharply. Decorate with the crystallized ginger or mini gingerbread men.

FROSTING VARIATIONS:

Cream cheese – ½ quantity cream cheese frosting from Gingerbread Layer Cake (see page 76)

Orange – Scatter with orange zest or add a little orange juice to the buttercream

Vanilla – Omit the chocolate and add a teaspoon of vanilla extract to the buttercream

Spiced – Add a pinch of ground ginger or cinnamon to the buttercream

PAIN D'EPICES
WITH CHOCOLATE SAUCE

SERVES 12 - PREP: 20 MINUTES, PLUS COOLING - COOK: 45 MINUTES

This is my take on the French classic "spice bread." Delicious on its own or spread with a little butter, but best served my way with a glossy chocolate orange sauce!

¾ cup honey

1 cup dark brown sugar

7 tablespoons unsalted butter, plus extra for greasing

3¼ cups all-purpose flour

1 teaspoon baking powder

1 teaspoon baking soda

½ teaspoon salt

2 teaspoons ground ginger

1 teaspoon ground cinnamon

1 teaspoon ground nutmeg

½ teaspoon ground cloves

½ cup ground almonds

zest of 1 lemon

3 large free-range eggs

¼ cup dark rum

1 teaspoon almond extract

FOR THE CHOCOLATE SAUCE

½ cup heavy cream

1 tablespoon dark brown sugar

2 tablespoons unsalted butter

1 tablespoon corn syrup

3 ounces dark chocolate (70% cocoa), finely chopped

1 tablespoon Cointreau

1. Put the honey, sugar, and butter in a medium saucepan and place over low heat. Melt together, stirring frequently, until the sugar has dissolved. Let cool for 15 minutes.

2. Preheat the oven to 325°F. Generously grease a 2-quart (8 x 4 inches) Bundt pan or an 8-inch round deep cake pan.

3. Sift the flour, baking powder, baking soda, salt, and spices into a large bowl. Fold in the ground almonds and lemon zest.

4. Pour the melted honey mixture into the flour mix and, using a handheld mixer, beat together. Add the eggs, rum, and almond extract and beat together until combined.

5. Pour into the greased pan and bake on the middle rack of the oven for 25 minutes before covering with a double layer of foil. Return to the oven for another 15 minutes or until a skewer emerges clean. Let cool for 15 minutes in the pan, then turn onto a wire rack to cool completely.

6. To make the chocolate sauce, put the cream, sugar, butter, and corn syrup in a small saucepan. Place over low/medium heat and stir until the sugar dissolves. Remove from the heat and stir in the chopped chocolate until melted and glossy. Finally, add the Cointreau and gently stir until combined.

7. Drizzle the hot sauce over the cake or serve separately.

APPLE & GINGERBREAD STREUSEL TART

MAKES 1 TART · PREP: 30 MINUTES, PLUS CHILLING · COOK: 40 MINUTES

The use of gingerbread in place of pastry dough in this happy blend of English apple crumble, Dutch apple pie, and German streusel makes it unlike other tarts you have had before.

½ x quantity of Dark Gingerbread Dough (see page 9)

FOR THE FILLING

2 (approx. ¾ pound) Macintosh apples, peeled and cored

3 (approx. 10½ ounces) medium apples, peeled and cored

juice of 1 lemon

⅓ cup granulated sugar

⅓ cup light brown sugar

3 tablespoons all-purpose flour

1 teaspoon ground cinnamon

¼ teaspoon ground allspice

½ teaspoon salt

½ cup golden raisins

1 tablespoon butter, cubed

FOR THE STREUSEL TOPPING

⅓ cup all-purpose flour

¼ cup granulated sugar

½ teaspoon ground ginger

pinch of salt

4 tablespoons cold butter, cut into small cubes

¼ cup pecans, coarsely chopped

1. Preheat the oven to 325°F. Cut a large piece of parchment paper and roll out the gingerbread on top of it to ¼-inch thick x 13-inch diameter. Line a deep 10-inch fluted pie dish with the dough. Press gently into the edges and trim any excess with a sharp knife. Reserve the trimmings. Place the crust in the freezer to chill for 20 minutes.

2. Meanwhile cut the apples into ¼-inch thick slices, squeeze over the lemon juice, then toss in a large bowl with the sugars, flour, spices, salt, and golden raisins.

3. Pile high into the chilled gingerbread crust, then press down to fill the gaps. Dot with the butter and place on a baking sheet to catch any spills. Bake for 20 minutes on the middle rack of the oven.

4. To make the streusel, mix the flour, sugar, ginger, and salt until combined. Cut 2 ounces of the reserved gingerbread dough into small chunks and add to the mix with the butter. Rub together with the tips of your fingers to form clumps. Stir in the pecans.

5. After the tart has baked for 20 minutes, sprinkle with the streusel and return to the oven to bake for another 30 minutes, or until the tart is golden and bubbling and the apples are tender when pierced with a sharp knife. Remove from the oven and set aside to cool slightly before serving. Alternatively, serve chilled.

GINGERBREAD KNOTS

MAKES: 12 - PREP: 45 MINUTES, PLUS COOLING & RISING - COOK: 20 MINUTES

This is a twist on the Swedish cinnamon buns that are scattered with crunchy pearl sugar. It's easy to make these look great—just twist up the dough and you're done!

1¼ cups whole milk

6 cardamom pods, husks removed and seeds ground

3 tablespoons butter

3¼ cups bread flour

1 tablespoon ground ginger

¼-ounce package fast-action yeast

¼ cup superfine sugar

½ teaspoon salt

2 large free-range eggs

1 tablespoon olive oil

¼ cup pearl sugar or sugar nibs (large grains of pure sugar that don't melt in the oven)

FOR THE GINGERBREAD FILLING

7 tablespoons salted butter, softened

⅓ cup dark brown sugar

zest of ½ orange

2 teaspoons ground ginger

1 teaspoon ground cinnamon

½ teaspoon ground nutmeg

¼ teaspoon ground cloves

½ teaspoon salt

1. Place the milk and ground cardamom seeds in a small saucepan and bring just to a boil. Remove from the heat and stir in the butter until melted. Set aside to reduce in temperature to lukewarm.

2. Meanwhile, sift the flour, ginger, yeast, superfine sugar, and salt into a bowl. Make a well in the center and mix in 1 egg. Once the milk is lukewarm, pour in the dry mixture and stir until it comes together to make a soft, sticky dough.

3. Knead for 10 minutes using an electric dough hook until it is smooth and springs back a little. If kneading by hand, transfer to an oiled surface and knead for 10 minutes. The dough will be very sticky to begin with, but do not add any additional flour. Transfer to a clean bowl greased with oil. Cover loosely with greased plastic wrap and leave in a warm place for 30 minutes until it has nearly doubled in size.

4. To make the filling, beat the butter, sugar, zest, spices, and salt together until soft and spreadable. Set aside.

5. Lightly flour a clean surface and dust your hands in flour. Tip out the dough, turn once to lightly coat in the flour, and divide it in half. Roll one piece into a large rectangle, about 16 x 20 inches. Spread half of the filling on top.

6. Fold one third of the dough over the second third. Then take the third piece and fold over the first and second piece. You will now have three layers of dough that look like how you would fold a letter. Cut the dough into 6 long strips approximately ¾-inch wide. Twist each strip together into a knot, tucking any ends underneath, and place evenly spread on a large baking sheet lined with a silicone baking sheet or parchment paper. Repeat with the remaining dough and

gingerbread filling and place on a second lined baking sheet.

7. Cover loosely with greased plastic wrap and leave once again in a warm place for 30 minutes until nearly doubled in size. Preheat the oven to 400°F. Brush very lightly with beaten egg and sprinkle with pearl sugar. Bake in the oven for 8 to 10 minutes, until lightly golden brown.

VARIATIONS

Chocoholic – Add 1 tablespoon of cocoa powder to the filling or 2 tablespoons to the dough! Yum!

Go nutty – Sprinkle ½ cup finely chopped pecans or hazelnuts over the filling before folding.

TIP For a consistent warm place to rise dough, place a bowl of boiling water in the base of a cold oven and place the dough bowl covered in plastic wrap at the top.

LEBKUCHEN

MAKES 24 - PREP: 45 MINUTES, PLUS COOLING & SETTING - COOK: 20 MINUTES

Lebkuchen is a German gingerbread that has become synonymous with Christmas baking. A cross between a cookie and cake with a delicious mixture of honey, almond, ginger, and cocoa, it is another frontrunner for edible gifts.

½ cup honey

8 tablespoons (1 stick) unsalted butter

½ cup ground almonds

2 cups all-purpose flour

½ teaspoon baking powder

¾ teaspoon baking soda

1 tablespoon ground ginger

2 teaspoons ground cinnamon

½ teaspoon ground nutmeg

¼ teaspoon ground cloves

2 teaspoons cocoa powder

¼ teaspoon salt

TO DECORATE

1¼ cups confectioners' sugar

1 large egg white

2 to 3 tablespoons cold water

3½ ounces dark chocolate, melted

YOU WILL NEED

a 1½-inch heart cutter

1. Melt the honey and butter in a small saucepan over low heat. Stir occasionally until combined. Remove from the heat and set aside to cool for 15 minutes.

2. Preheat the oven to 325°F. Line 2 large baking sheets with silicone baking sheets or parchment paper.

3. Place the ground almonds in a large bowl and sift in the remaining ingredients. Pour in the cooled honey mixture and stir until it comes together to make a dough.

4. Divide the dough and set one half aside. Roll the other half into small equal balls, place on a lined baking sheet, and press each one down slightly with the palm of your hand to approx. ¾-inch thick.

5. Roll out the remaining dough to ¾-inch thick and, using a 1½-inch heart cutter, cut into cookies. Soften the edges of the hearts with your fingers. Place on the other lined baking sheet. Bake in the oven for 8 to 10 minutes, until just golden brown at the edges. Let cool for 5 minutes on the pans, then transfer to wire racks to cool completely.

6. Meanwhile, mix the confectioners' sugar, egg white, and water together to make a thin, runny icing. Place a baking sheet under the wire rack and thinly brush the lebkuchen with the icing using a pastry brush. Leave for 15 minutes to set, then repeat with the remaining icing. Let set.

7. Dip half of the lebkuchen into the melted chocolate to coat the base and just barely up the side. Then drizzle the remaining half with a zig-zag of chocolate.

TIP These cookies really do improve with age, that's if you can bear to wait, and you must!

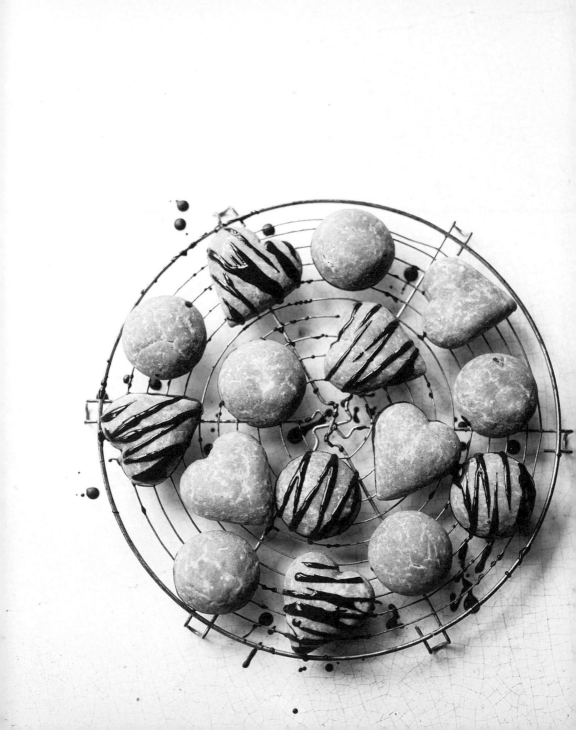

INGREDIENTS IN A JAR GIFT
CHEWY GINGERBREAD COOKIES

MAKES 1 QUART JAR/22 COOKIES - PREP: 15 MINUTES, PLUS CHILLING - COOK: 10 MINUTES

This is such a fun gift to give friends. You can mix up the spices, chocolate chips, and crystallized ginger to make different flavored cookies.

1⅔ cups all-purpose flour

1 teaspoon baking powder

1 teaspoon baking soda

½ teaspoon salt

½ cup brown sugar

2 teaspoons ground ginger

1 teaspoon ground cinnamon

½ teaspoon ground nutmeg

¼ teaspoon ground cloves

1¼ cups rolled oats

½ cup white chocolate chips

½ cup crystallized ginger, finely chopped

YOU WILL NEED

a 1-quart jar

IF MAKING THE COOKIES YOURSELF YOU WILL ALSO NEED

8 tablespoons (1 stick) unsalted butter

⅓ cup dark or blackstrap molasses

¼ cup corn syrup/honey

1 large free-range egg, lightly beaten

To make a layered jar:

1. Pack each layer down tightly into the jar, pressing with your fist or the back of a spoon. You will need to pack it in well or the ingredients will not fit. Leave a few oats out if there isn't space.

First - flour, baking powder, baking soda, and salt
Second - brown sugar
Third - spices
Fourth - oats
Fifth - chocolate chips
Sixth - crystallized ginger

2. Make a label giving the following instructions:

You will need: 8 tablespoons (1 stick) unsalted butter, ⅓ cup dark molasses, ¼ cup corn syrup, and 1 large egg.

In a large saucepan, melt the butter, molasses, and corn syrup together until combined. Let cool for 5 minutes, then pour the contents of the jar into the saucepan and mix together with the beaten egg until combined.

Roll the dough into 1½-inch balls and place on lined baking sheets approx. 1½ inch apart. Chill in the fridge for 20 minutes.

Preheat the oven to 325°F. Bake for 10 minutes, until the surface has cracked. Let cool for 5 minutes on the pans, then transfer to wire racks to cool completely.

If you are making the cookies yourself, use the fresh ingredients listed and follow the same directions you would write on a label!

GINGERBREAD SYRUP

MAKES 1¼ CUPS- PREP: 10 MINUTES, PLUS COOLING - COOK 20 TO 25 MINUTES

The aroma alone of warming spices can lure you into a coffee shop for a gingerbread latte or a spiced hot chocolate. Now you can enjoy it at home! Just add a tablespoon to your mug before pouring in your hot drink of choice.

1½ cups granulated sugar

1 tablespoon ground ginger

2 teaspoons ground cinnamon

1 teaspoon ground nutmeg

¼ teaspoon ground cloves

¼ teaspoon salt

½ teaspoon vanilla extract

1. Put 2 cups water in a large, heavy-bottomed saucepan with the sugar, spices, and salt and bring to a boil. Watch carefully or the mixture may overflow.

2. Reduce to a rolling simmer and cook for 15 to 20 minutes uncovered, or until the consistency of maple syrup. Remove from the heat and stir in the vanilla. Let cool completely.

3. Transfer to a jar or bottle, seal with a lid, and store in the fridge for up to 1 month. If your syrup crystallizes over time re-liquify in a bain marie.

TIP Add a dash to your latte, hot chocolate, pancakes, oatmeal, or even cocktails!

TOWN HOUSE

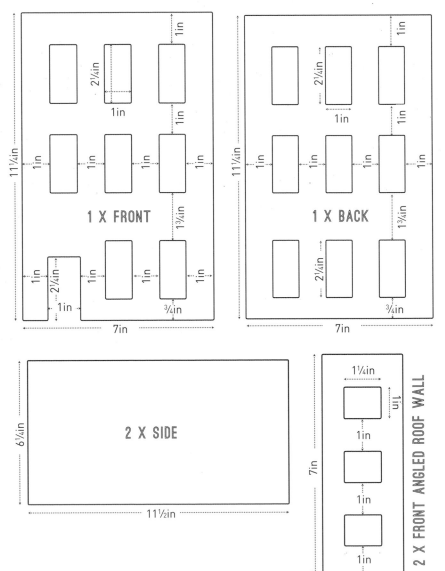

1 X FRONT

1 X BACK

2 X SIDE

2 X FRONT ANGLED ROOF WALL

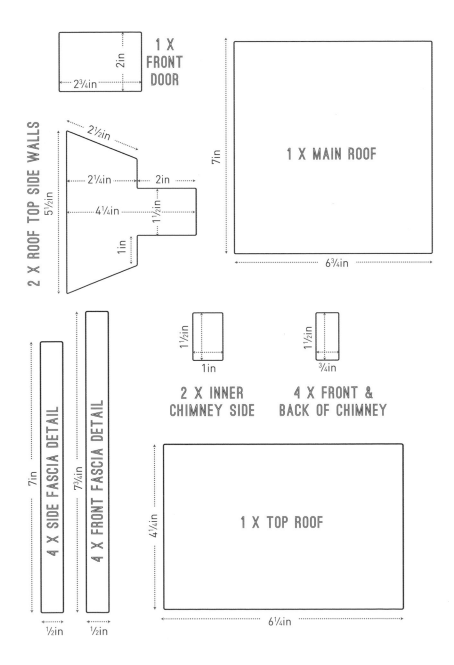

1 X FRONT DOOR

2in

2¾in

2 X ROOF TOP SIDE WALLS

2½in

2¼in

2in

5½in

4¼in

1½in

1in

1 X MAIN ROOF

7in

6¾in

2 X INNER CHIMNEY SIDE

1½in

1in

4 X FRONT & BACK OF CHIMNEY

1½in

¾in

4 X SIDE FASCIA DETAIL

7in

½in

4 X FRONT FASCIA DETAIL

7¾in

½in

1 X TOP ROOF

4¼in

6¼in

HOLLY ROOF HOUSE

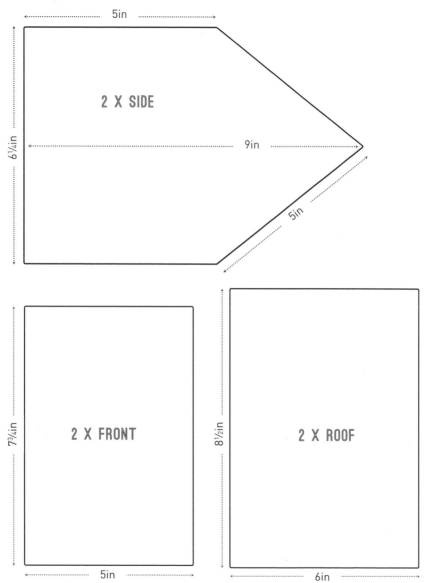

2 X SIDE

5in

6¼in

9in

5in

2 X FRONT

7¾in

5in

2 X ROOF

8½in

6in

GINGER BREAD STREET 1

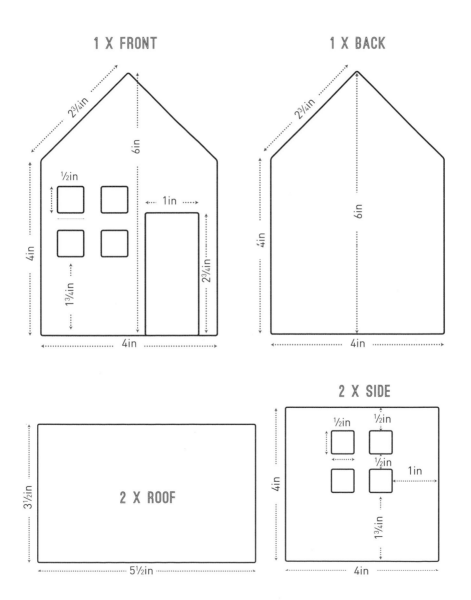

GINGER BREAD STREET 2

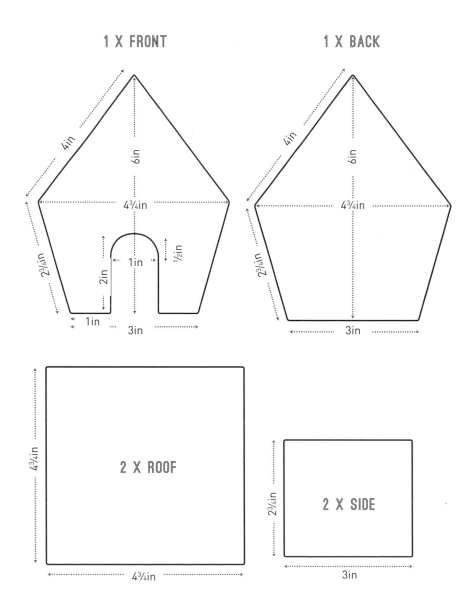

1 X FRONT

1 X BACK

4in

6in

4¾in

2in

1in

½in

2in

2¾in

1in

3in

4in

6in

4¾in

2¾in

3in

2 X ROOF

4¾in

4¾in

2 X SIDE

2¾in

3in

GINGER BREAD STREET 3

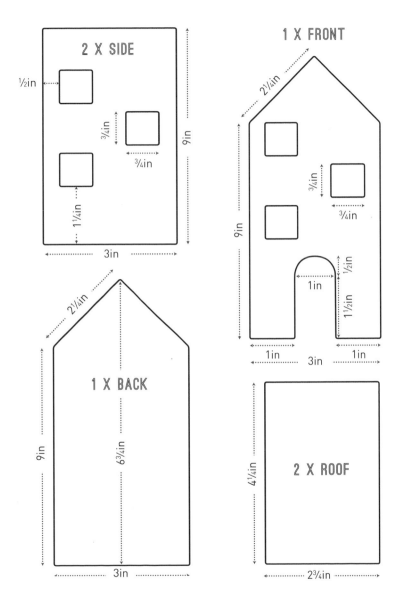

2 X SIDE

½in

¾in

¾in

1¼in

9in

3in

1 X FRONT

2¼in

¾in

¾in

9in

½in

1in

1½in

1in

3in

1in

1 X BACK

2¼in

9in

6¾in

3in

2 X ROOF

4¼in

2¾in

HANSEL AND GRETEL HOUSE

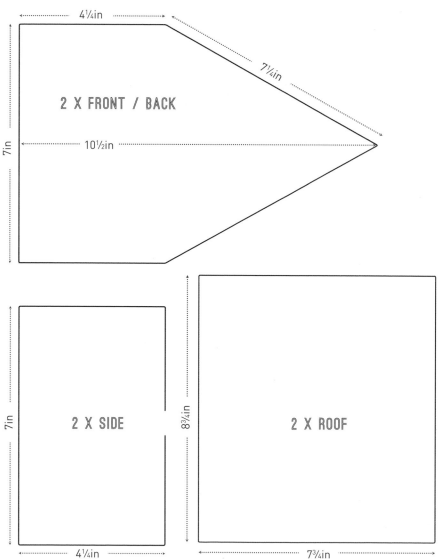

2 X FRONT / BACK

4¼in

7¼in

7in

10½in

2 X SIDE

7in

4¼in

2 X ROOF

8¾in

7¾in

COUNTRY COTTAGE

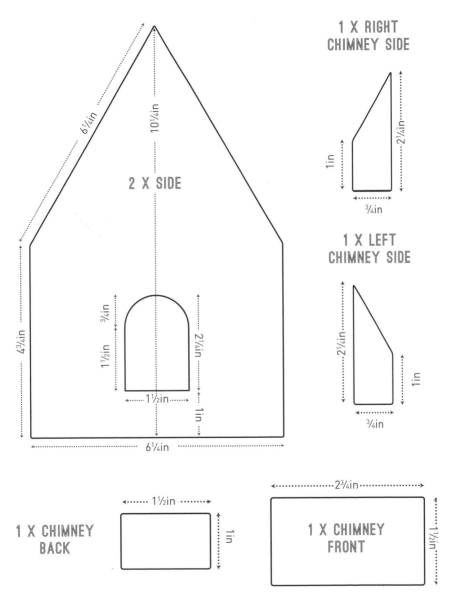

1 X RIGHT
CHIMNEY SIDE

2 X SIDE

6¼in

10¼in

4¾in

¾in

1½in

2¼in

1in

1½in

6¼in

2¼in

¾in

1in

1 X LEFT
CHIMNEY SIDE

2¼in

¾in

1in

1 X CHIMNEY
BACK

1½in

1in

2¾in

1 X CHIMNEY
FRONT

1½in

COUNTRY COTTAGE CONTINUED

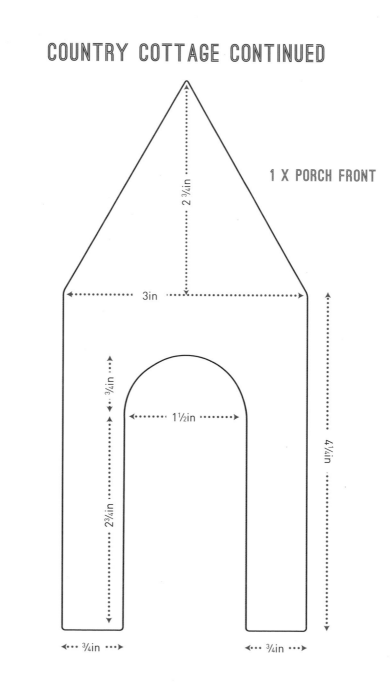

1 X PORCH FRONT

2 ¾in

3in

¾in

4¼in

1½in

2¾in

¾in

¾in

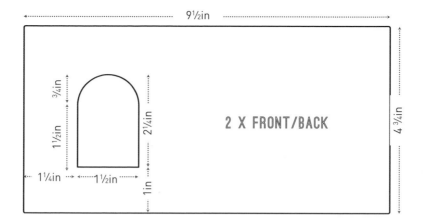

9½in

¾in

1½in

2¼in

1¼in

1½in

1in

4 ¾in

2 X FRONT/BACK

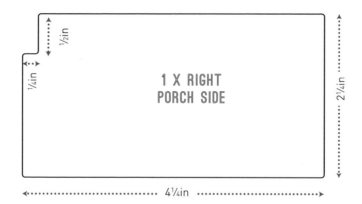

½in

¼in

1 X RIGHT
PORCH SIDE

2¼in

4¼in

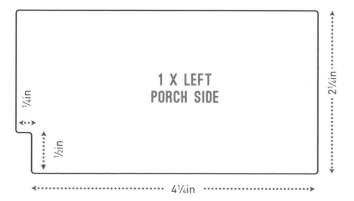

¼in

½in

1 X LEFT
PORCH SIDE

2¼in

4¼in

COUNTRY COTTAGE CONTINUED

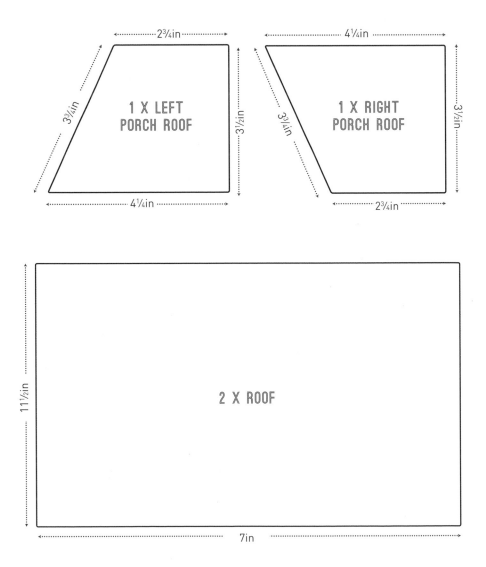

2¾in

3¾in

1 X LEFT
PORCH ROOF

3½in

4¼in

4¼in

3¾in

1 X RIGHT
PORCH ROOF

3½in

2¾in

11½in

2 X ROOF

7in

MINI MUG GINGERBREAD HOUSE

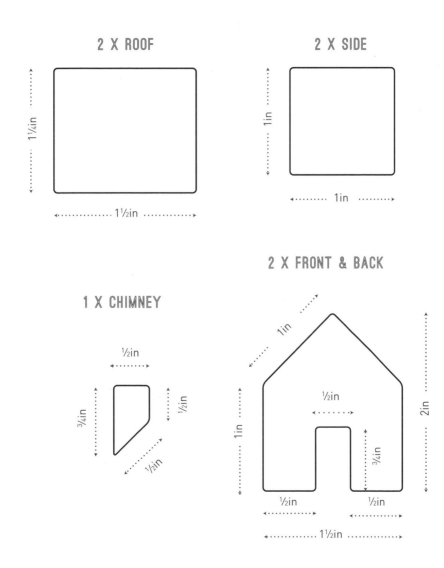

2 X ROOF

1¼in

1½in

2 X SIDE

1in

1in

1 X CHIMNEY

½in

¾in

½in

½in

2 X FRONT & BACK

1in

½in

1in

¾in

2in

½in

½in

1½in

BIRD HOUSE

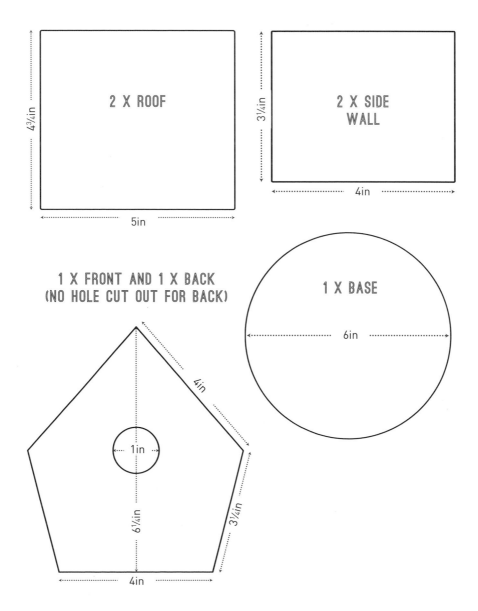

2 X ROOF

4¾in

5in

2 X SIDE WALL

3¼in

4in

1 X FRONT AND 1 X BACK
(NO HOLE CUT OUT FOR BACK)

1in

4in

6¼in

3¼in

4in

1 X BASE

6in

3D CHRISTMAS TREES

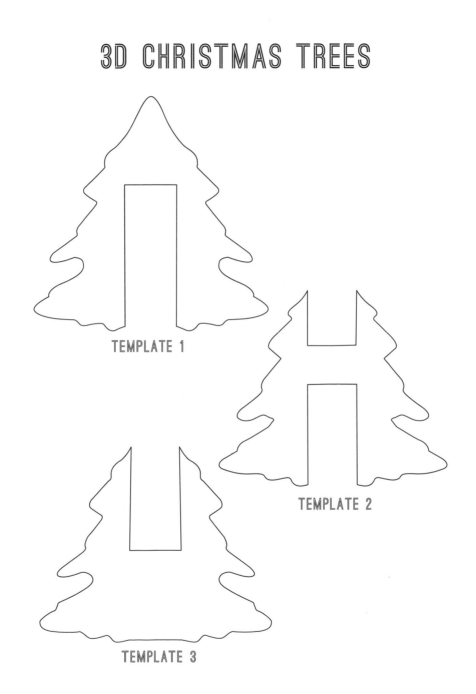

TEMPLATE 1

TEMPLATE 2

TEMPLATE 3

INDEX

THANK YOU

Many very talented people would give just about anything to have their own cookbook published, so I feel overwhelmingly grateful to have been able to write my second book so soon after my first.

Some people gave their time, effort, advice, and support, others just ate lots of gingerbread so I didn't have to look at the increasing piles any longer. Thank you to everyone; however big or small you think your efforts were, they were huge to me.

To Kyle and Judith, thank you for believing in me a second time. Your enthusiasm for new projects is infectious.

To Sophie, Judith, and Hannah, thank you for your organization— the work you juggle on a daily basis is really quite impressive. Your advice, support, and flexibility have been invaluable to me, but it's your humor that is the key to keeping everything running smoothly!

To Tara, you effortlessly captured the magic that surrounds gingerbread. You produce the most beautiful images one after the other and I love each new photograph more than the last.

To Tabitha, you see the world in such a beautiful way and you have brought that beauty to life in the pages of this book.

To Anita, you have given this book the style I struggled to get into words when we started. I couldn't have imagined it better myself.

What a wonderful and inspiring group of ladies. Thank you for putting your hearts into it and for making the shoot days such a pleasure. Who said work wasn't fun?

And to Tom. For putting up with what felt like a whole street of gingerbread houses on the dining table and for laughing when I opened a drawer to rest yet another pan of cookies on when I found that every other surface in the flat was already taken. Your laughter and support is something I will always cherish.

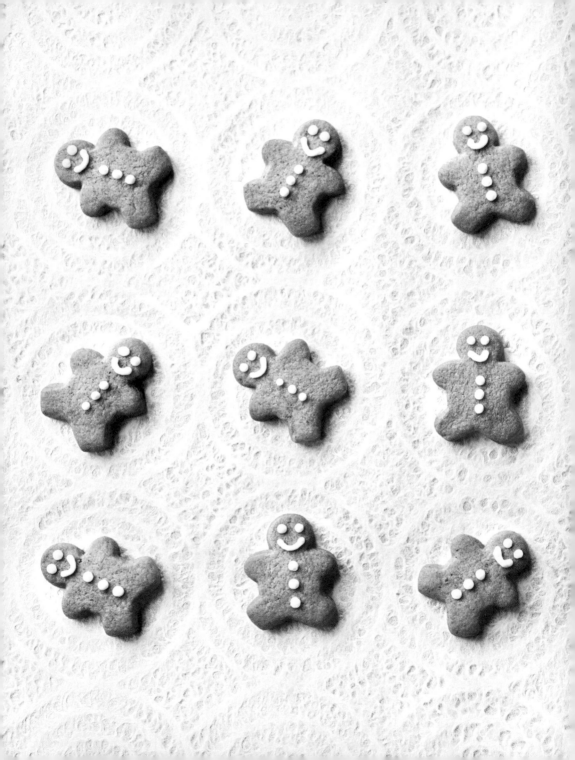